MEDIEVAL CHRISTIANITY

Christopher Dawson

1935

CATHOLIC TRUTH SOCIETY

PUBLISHERS TO THE HOLY SEE

Christopher Dawson (1889-1970), a convert from Anglicanism, was a historian of religion and culture.

CTS ONEFIFTIES

Originally published 1935; with updated bibliography, 1961.

Published by The Incorporated Catholic Truth Society,

40-46 Harleyford Road, London SE11 5AY

www.ctsbooks.org

All rights reserved.

Copyright © 2017 The Incorporated Catholic Truth Society.

ISBN 978 1 78469 544 6

It was the most creative age
of European history…Out of the
chaos of barbarian tribes
and the debris of the Roman Empire,
it created a Christian people.

MEDIEVAL CHRISTIANITY

CHRISTOPHER DAWSON

The subject of this study is the thousand years of religious development from the fall of the Roman Empire in the west to the Reformation. People often speak and write of mediæval religion and the mediæval Church as though they were simple and uniform phenomena. Actually this is very far from being the case. They do not remember that the distance that separated the end of the Middle Ages from their beginning is twice as long as that which divides the age of Lenin from that of Joan of Arc, or the age of the Maccabees from the age of the Fathers. The 1,000 years in question were a period of intense cultural and spiritual change. They saw the creation of Europe and the birth of modern western civilization. When they began Northern Europe was still pagan and barbarous, and the centre of civilization and of Christianity was in the Eastern Mediterranean and to a large extent outside the frontiers of Europe. When they ended South-eastern Europe was being overrun by the Turk, and America was being conquered by the Christians. And how much had happened in the meantime! The conversion of the West, the brilliant dawn of Celtic and Anglo-Saxon Christianity, the rise of Islam and the ruin of the great churches of Africa and Egypt and Syria, the conversion of the Germans and the Slavs, and the formation of the Holy Roman Empire, the conflict between the Papacy and the Empire, the Crusades, the formation of the universities and the rise of scholasticism, the great movement of mediæval monasticism—the Cluniacs, the Cistercians, the Franciscans, and the Dominicans—the growth of the national monarchies, the Great Schism and the Conciliar movement, the fall of the Byzantine Empire and the beginnings of the Renaissance. All these movements and events are part of the history of mediæval Christendom, and each affords sufficient material for a book—indeed for a number of books.

EAST AND WEST

Here we must limit ourselves to considering briefly some of the main aspects of the religious development of western Christendom. It is, however, important for us to remember that this is only a part of the subject. Mediæval Christianity was not wholly western and not exclusively Catholic. At the same time that England was being converted by the Benedictines and the Irish monks, Nestorian missionaries were carrying Christianity to China; and while Scandinavia was becoming Catholic, Russia was receiving its Christianity from the Byzantine Empire at the very time when it was drifting into permanent schism with the West. There were flourishing Christian cultures in mediæval Armenia and Georgia, and Abyssinia remained a lonely outpost of Monophysite Christianity far away in the East African highlands. The problem of reunion was a vital issue all through the later Middle Ages down to the Council of Florence in 1438-45,[1] while the vague consciousness of the lost Nestorian Christianity of Central Asia embodied itself in the legendary figure of Prester John, the priest king of a mysterious realm in the Far East.[2] One of the strangest and most romantic episodes in the story of mediæval Christendom is that of the embassy of the Nestorian monk, Rabban Sauma, who travelled from Pekin to Rome at the close of the thirteenth century, and who has left us an eye-witness's account

---

[1] *Cf.* Norden *Papstum und Byzanz.*
[2] Probably the Nestorian Uighur Turk kingdom of the Kerait in Central Asia. See *The Mongol Mission*, ed. Dawson, 1955 (The Makers of Christendom Series).

of western Christendom as it appeared to a Christian from China.[1]

Such episodes are rare. During the greater part of the Middle Ages, western Christendom was shut off from the rest of the world by the unbreakable barrier of Islam, and the Mediterranean, the old highway of civilization, was, especially in its western half, closed to Christian shipping. Nevertheless, there was much more intercourse between East and West than we might have expected. The first Archbishop of Canterbury was a Greek from Cilicia. At a later period western scholars, like Adelard of Bath, learnt their science from Jewish and Arabic masters in Spain and in the East, while, still later, the Franciscan missionaries penetrated to China and India, and Greek monks and bishops, like Barlaam of Calabria and the great Bessarion, brought back the knowledge of Greek literature to the Latin world.

But above all we must remember that the whole Christian culture of the mediæval world was built upon non-European foundations. The spiritual masters of the Middle Ages were the monks of the Egyptian desert and the African St Augustine; their intellectual teachers were (apart from St Augustine) the Fathers of the Eastern Church, above all the great Cappadocians, Basil, and the two Gregories,

---

[1] Translation by E. A. Wallis Budge, in *The Monks of Kublai Khan*, 1928.

and the Syrian, Eusebius, the results of whose labours were communicated to the west through the medium of the writings of Ambrose and Jerome and Rufinus.

When the Roman Empire lost the western provinces, the main centres of Christian thought and culture, and the majority of the Christian population were still outside Europe—in North Africa and Egypt, in Syria and Asia Minor, in Mesopotamia and Armenia. At the end of the Middle Ages the geographical situation of Christianity in the old world was much the same as we find it to-day: it had become a European religion with its centre in the West, and had lost its hold on Western Asia and North Africa, where it had formerly been so flourishing.

THE MAIN PHASES OF THE MEDIÆVAL CHRISTIAN DEVELOPMENT

The essence of the mediæval development consists in this reception of Christianity by the West, the conversion of the northern peoples and the building of a new Christian culture on the old religious foundations but with new social and racial elements. Thus the history of the Middle Ages falls naturally into two halves—the age of the conversion of the

Barbarians, which is often spoken of as "The Dark Ages," and the age of the revival of western culture, from the eleventh to the fifteenth centuries, which is the great age of mediæval Christendom and of mediæval civilization.

It is, however, impossible to understand mediæval religion if we isolate it from the age that has gone before. The age of the Fathers—the Patristic age—is the foundation of the whole mediæval development. In some respects it may even be regarded as an organic part of that development. Hence, though this age has already been dealt with in the preceding essay by Father Philip Hughes from the oriental point of view—that is to say, with reference to the Byzantine Empire and the great oriental heresies, it is necessary to say something further about it here from the occidental point of view and with reference to the new situation which arose for the Church in the West with the fall of the Empire and the coming of the barbarian kingdoms.

1. THE PATRISTIC AGE AND THE CHURCH IN THE WEST

We have already seen that the main centres of Christian culture at this period were in the East and in Africa. In the West, at least in the European West, paganism was still strong, and the educated classes were still largely non-Christian in sentiment and culture. The great councils, the great theological schools, and the great monastic centres were all in Asia and Africa, and the chief task before the western Church was to assimilate and transmit this ecclesiastical culture with its theological science and its forms of monastic life to the provinces of Western Europe. But this task was not finished when disaster overtook the Western Empire. The fall of Rome inspired one of the greatest of St Augustine's works, the "City of God," and his own church and fatherland were being devastated by the barbarians while he lay dying at Hippo. Thus the western Church had to face a double labour. On the one hand she had to protect her flock from the barbarians and spread the Gospel among the latter, while on the other she had to carry on the tradition of patristic culture inaugurated by St Hilary, St Ambrose, and St Jerome. This double function is seen in the work of St Leo, the greatest Pope of the Patristic Age, who, on the one hand, was obliged to take a leading part in the theological struggles of the Eastern Empire, while at the same time he had to protect Rome from the Huns and strengthen the discipline of the western Church amid the social dissolution of the barbarian invasions.

There has never been a time when a heavier social responsibility fell upon the Church, for she alone was left to come to the rescue of humanity and to alleviate the immense suffering and distress of the conquered populations; and nobly was the task fulfilled by the great Popes and Bishops of the time—the last of the Romans—men like St Leo and St Germanus of Auxerre, St Sidonius Apollinaris, Bishop and Poet, St Remigius of Rheims, the apostle of the Franks, and St Cæsarius of Arles. Nor did the bishops stand alone. Among the great religious figures of the age there were women like St Genevieve, the Saint of Paris, whose heroic faith protected the city in the dark days of the invasions and the Frankish conquest, while in Britain we have St Patrick, who out of the ruin of his country and his own captivity and slavery conquered, almost single-handed, a new nation for Christ.

2. THE DARK AGES AND THE CONVERSION OF THE BARBARIANS

With the writings of St Patrick, so lacking in theological science or classical culture, yet at the same time so original and so sincere, we seem already to have entered the mediæval world. It is indeed difficult to say where the Patristic Age ends and where the Middle Ages begin. For the Dark Ages had already begun in Britain and Roman Germany and Northern Gaul, while Italy and

Africa still formed part of the Roman-Byzantine world. Perhaps we cannot do better than to take the Pontificate of St Gregory the Great (590-604) as the landmark between two ages, for while he belongs by birth and tradition to the old Roman world, his figure dominates the Catholicism of the succeeding age in a most striking way.

St Gregory was not a great original thinker like St Augustine, in spite of the immense influence of his thought on that of the mediæval world. He was not a great man of letters, like St Jerome, though he was the favourite author of the mediæval Church. But he was emphatically a great man—great in his faith and great in his works. When we read his letters, and see him struggling single-handed against the Lombards as the representative of the Empire and of civilization, against the imperial government itself as the champion of justice and humanity, and against famine and pestilence and economic ruin as the last remaining refuge of the people of Italy, we realize the heroic and almost superhuman character of his life work. In such an age of universal ruin and despair, it would have been easy for him to withdraw from the world and to give himself up to the contemplative life which had so strong an appeal for his mind, as we see in those famous Dialogues in the composition of which he found refuge and relaxation. But instead of making other-worldliness an excuse for inaction, he made it the basis of his activity and the reservoir from which he drew his resources of spiritual energy. And thus his pontificate was not, as he supposed, the end of the old world, but a turning point in the history of civilization and the beginning of a new movement of Catholic expansion. The following centuries saw the conversion of England, the conversion of Germany, the reform of the Frankish Church, and finally the conversion of Scandinavia. In a word, it was the age of the formation of western Christendom; and thus, in spite of its barbarism and material failure, it was the most creative age in European history. Its achievement was a purely religious one, represented by the figures of the great monastic missionaries, like the two Columbas, St Wilfred and St Boniface, St Ansgar and St Adalbert, and by the monastic scholars, Bede and Alcuin, Rabanus Maurus, and Paschasius Radbertus. But this religious achievement was also a social and cultural one; for it made Europe. Out of the chaos of barbarian tribes and the debris of the Roman Empire, it created a Christian people and, in the words of Gibbon, "gradually produced the similar manners and common jurisprudence which have distinguished, from the rest of mankind, the independent and even hostile nations of modern Europe."[1]

3. MEDIÆVAL CHRISTENDOM AND THE REVIVAL OF WESTERN CULTURE

On these foundations there was built the civilization which we are accustomed to describe as "mediæval." The achievement of the later Middle Ages from the eleventh to the fifteenth century really deserves the name of a "Renaissance" better than the more limited movement to which the name has been appropriated. These centuries, especially the twelfth and the thirteenth, witnessed a most remarkable revival of cultural activity in every field, intellectual, political, and economic. It saw the building of the great cathedral and monastic houses, the foundation of the Communes and the Universities, the development of canon law, scholastic philosophy, and vernacular literature. For our present purpose, at any rate, the most significant thing about this movement is that it was inspired and moulded by religious forces. It was the Church rather than the State which took the lead in the revival of western civilization, and every aspect of that revival, even the political and economic ones, tended to assume religious forms. Thus the economic revival

---

[1] *History of the Decline and Fall of the Roman Empire*, ch. xxxvii., ii. The Conversion of the Barbarians.

was largely based on religious forms of association, such as the confraternity and "charity"; and the communal movement, both in North Italy and in Northern Europe, was often closely associated with the movement of ecclesiastical reform. Even the warlike energies of European society found an explicitly religious outlet in the Crusades, which are in some respects the most typical feature of the new age, since they are peculiar to it and are equally foreign to the religion of the preceding period and to that of the age which followed.

The very idea of a religious war is apt to shock the modern mind, but we cannot understand mediæval religion, at least in its more popular aspects, unless we realize the strength of the religious emotion which drove so many myriads of Christians to take the Cross and to leave their bones on the long road through Asia Minor, or to rot in the prisons of Egypt and Syria. The significant thing about the Crusading movement is that it was an attempt to Christianize mediæval society in its most vital but least Christian aspect, and thus it denotes a real fusion between the native tradition of the warrior peoples of Western Europe and the ideals of the Church and the Christian tradition. We see in early mediæval literature—for example, in the Chansons de Geste—how wide was the gulf between these two traditions and how much of the leaven of pagan barbarism still remained in the feudal society of the twelfth century. Yet in the following century the Crusading ideal finds expression in the life of St Louis, which is one of the noblest examples of mediæval religion.[1] Here the leaven of paganism is entirely purged away, while the characteristic heroic idealism of the northern warrior tradition remains.

But while the Crusades are the most characteristic feature of the religious life of the times, they are far inferior in intrinsic importance to the great movement of ecclesiastical reform and religious revival which is the key to the history of the mediæval Church. The fall of the Roman Empire in the west, and the conversion of the barbarians, had had a profound influence on the social structure and economic organization of the Church. It had ceased to be the Church of the cities, as it had been in the patristic period, and had become rural and agrarian. Bishops and abbots had become great landowners, with an immense subject population dependent upon them. The rulers of the barbarian kingdoms, Franks, Anglo-Saxons, and Visigoths, found the Church an invaluable ally in the task of government, and made the bishops their councillors

---

[1]There is an English translation of the *Life of St Louis*, by Joinville, in Everyman's Library. The same volume contains Villehardouin's chronicle of the Fourth Crusade, which shows the reverse side of the movement. See also *The Life of St Louis*, trans. by R. Hayne, 1955 (The Makers of Christendom Series).

and ministers. Thus, for example, in Spain the ecclesiastical councils of Toledo became genuine national assemblies with legislative functions, while in England the bishops formed an important part of the Witan or royal council, and the kings and great men were present at the ecclesiastical councils and signed their decrees. This union of Church and State was carried even further in the Christian Empire of Charlemagne and his successors. The bishops were treated as imperial functionaries and took no less a part than the secular counts in the government and administration of the Empire. Finally, this process reached its climax in the 10th century in the restored Empire of Otto I and his successors. The German emperors made the bishops the corner-stone of their system of government, so that the latter combined with their episcopal office the secular office of the count and the secular privileges and responsibilities that went with it. Thus there arose the anomalous figure of the prince-bishop who governed his territories and made peace and war like any other feudal noble, and whose dual position and functions were an endless source of difficulty and friction alike to the mediæval Church and the mediæval State.

This state of things was felt to be intolerable by the more spiritually-minded element in the Church, which looked back with longing to the golden age of the Fathers and the primitive Church. Thus there arose a reforming movement which, beginning in the monasteries of Burgundy and Lorraine in the tenth century, gradually spread throughout the western Church. In the second half of the eleventh century this movement found its natural leader in the Papacy, and there began that great struggle between the Papacy and the Empire regarding the rights of the State in the appointment and control of the episcopate, which is known as the Investiture controversy. Although it proved impossible to carry out the full programme of reform and to desecularize the Church of the Empire completely, a real revolution took place in the ecclesiastical organization of western Christendom. The international unity of the Church under the authority of the Holy See was transformed from a theory into a reality. The loose federation of provinces and national churches, which had existed in the tenth century, gave place to a centralization of authority and jurisdiction which left little power to the Metropolitans and brought every part of Christendom into immediate relations with Rome. The development of the Curia and the Papal Chancery provided the Church with a constitutional and bureaucratic organization far in advance of the contemporary feudal state, while the institution of papal legates gave the Papacy the power to supervise the behaviour of the local ecclesiastical authorities and to intervene decisively in political affairs whenever the interests of the Church were in question. Above all, the new system of canon law, which was created by the movement of reform and by the great Popes of the eleventh and twelfth centuries, supplied a firm juridical basis for the international order of the reformed Church. This development of canon law and scientific ecclesiastical jurisprudence, which had its centre in the University of Bologna, was hardly less important for the history of the mediæval Church than was the philosophical and theological movement which had its centre in the University of Paris. Indeed, as de Ghellinck has shown, it was not without its influence on the latter, for in the twelfth century, the age of Gratian and Peter Lombard, theology and canon law still overlapped one another, and dealt to some extent with the same subject matter.[1]

All this work of constitutional and juridical organization was, however, only one side—the external side—of the movement of reform. To those who concentrate their attention on this aspect alone mediæval religion must inevitably appear external and legalistic, an affair of obligations and sanctions.[2]

[1] See P. Fournier and G. le Bras, *Histoire des collections canoniques depuis les Fausses Décretales jusqu'au Décret de Gratien*, 2 vols., 1931-2.
[2] *Cf.* for example the generalisation of the editors of the *Cambridge Mediæval History*, vol. vii., p. 20, "Christian doctrine from 1100 to 1300 had grown steadily legalised."

But there is also the interior side of the movement, which the reformers themselves regarded as its true end and *raison d'être*.

Now if we view mediæval religion in this aspect we shall see that its dominant tendency was not to exteriorize religion, but just the opposite—to humanize and interiorize it. Byzantine religion had developed the transcendent side of Christianity. It had emphasized the divine nature of Christ, the Uncreated Word, rather than the Divine Humanity. That is why the greater part of Oriental Christendom, Syria and Egypt, Armenia and Abyssinia, fell away from orthodoxy by a denial of the Human Nature of Christ and adopted the errors of Monophysitism. Mediæval Catholicism, on the other hand, concentrated its attention on the Humanity of Jesus, on the contemplation of His Life and Passion, and on the practice of the Imitation of Christ. These are the characteristic notes of mediæval religion from the time of the reforming movement down to the Protestant Reformation, from St Anselm and St Bernard to St Francis and St Bonaventure, to the Yorkshire hermit, Richard Rolle, and to Thomas a Kempis. St Bernard is perhaps the greatest of these "doctors of the sacred Humanity," and no single personality is more characteristic of mediæval religion, both in thought and action. It is, however, in St Francis that mediæval religion finds its most sublime expression, and one which makes a unique appeal not only to the mediæval mind but also to that of modern times. And the secret of this appeal is to be found precisely in the Christo-centric character of the life and doctrine of St Francis. What impressed his contemporaries and still impresses us to-day is the "conformity" of St Francis to the pattern of the Divine Humanity, so that, in the words of a mediæval writer,[1] "St Francis became as it were the *picture of Christ*, and was transformed at all points into Jesus, the Lord Himself completing and finishing this work by the impression of the stigmata."

But St Francis was not only a master of the spiritual life, he was also among the greatest of the leaders of the reforming movement, and his order, together with that of St Dominic, were the most efficient and devoted agents of the Papacy in its universal mission.

Unfortunately, the left wing of the Franciscan order, the so-called "Spirituals," developed revolutionary tendencies, which brought them into conflict with orthodox Catholic tradition and with the authority of the Holy See. This weakened both the reforming movement as a whole, and especially that alliance of the spiritual reformers

---

[1] The author of the *Meditationes vitæ Christi*, which were falsely attributed to St Bonaventure (John de Caulibus?).

and the Papacy which had been the basis of the whole religious movement from the eleventh to the thirteenth centuries. At the same time the growth of nationalism destroyed the international unity of mediæval culture and prepared the way for that great schism between Northern and Southern Europe which came to a head at the Reformation. The last two centuries of the Middle Ages saw the gradual disintegration of the unity that had been built up in the previous age. The spiritual vitality of mediæval religion was still strong, but it had lost its centre of unity and its constructive power. The last great attempt to reform the Church and to restore the unity of Christendom—the Conciliar movement—was a failure because it based its action on a kind of ecclesiastical constitutionalism which was inconsistent with the divine authority of the Holy See. Thus the Papacy, deserted by the reformers and opposed by a strong Gallicanizing movement, was forced to make its own terms with the new secular powers, and became itself increasingly absorbed in the secular politics and humanist culture of Renaissance Italy.

It was indeed at Rome that the Middle Ages first came to an end. Already in the first half of the fifteenth century, the age of St Joan, the Curia was thronged with bright young men who regarded the whole mediæval development as an unfortunate episode that was best forgotten, and who looked back to pagan antiquity with romantic enthusiasm.[1] More than a century was to pass before the old alliance of the Papacy and the spiritual reformers was renewed by St Ignatius and the heroes of the Counter-Reformation. But in the meantime the great revolt had taken place and Northern Europe had ceased to be Catholic.

To sum up the mediæval development, we may say that its essential characteristic is to be found in the transmission to the young peoples of Northern and Western Europe of the Catholic tradition, as formed by the Patristic age and the late Roman culture, and in the gradual process of assimilation that followed. In every manifestation of mediæval religion we can trace the interaction of these two factors. Thus mediæval religion is not simply Catholicism, it is Catholicism as expressed through a particular medium, a stubborn and resistant medium which often refuses to be moulded into Christian forms. There is, therefore, much in mediæval religion which belongs not so much to the Catholic tradition as to the other native or barbaric element that underlies mediæval culture, just as there is also much in it which

---

[1]The earliest and perhaps the most influential of these was the Florentine, Poggio Bracciolini (1380-1459), who spent the greater part of his life in the service of the Curia.

is not specifically mediæval but simply Catholic. Hence that revolt against mediæval culture, which is the Renaissance, is by no means to be identified with that revolt against mediæval Catholicism which is the Reformation. Wycliffe is a thoroughly mediæval man, but he is already more than half a Protestant, while his contemporary Colluccio Salutati was Catholic without being mediæval. When the religious revolt came, it came from the Gothic North, not from the classical South. Luther himself was hardly less mediæval than Wycliffe, whereas the Rome against which he revolted had been saturated by the influence of the Renaissance for a century, and was now the citadel of the new culture. Nevertheless, while recognising that what is Catholic is not necessarily mediæval, and what is mediæval is not necessarily Catholic, we must at the same time admit that there has never been an age in which European culture was more penetrated by the Catholic tradition, or in which Catholic ideals found a fuller expression in almost every field of human activity. The age of St Bernard and St Francis, of St Thomas and St Bonaventure, of St Louis and Dante, is perhaps the one age in which all that was strongest and most living in the European thought and society accepted Catholic principles and consecrated themselves to the service of God and His Church. Hence the positive achievements of mediæval religion have been incorporated into the Catholic tradition and have become part of the Church's spiritual patrimony. We see this in every side of Catholic life; in theology and philosophy, in organization and canon law, in liturgy and worship. One of the most important of these subjects—Scholasticism—has been dealt with at length in a separate essay, and I will now say something about the remaining aspects of mediæval religion and the contribution that they have made to the Catholic tradition.

4. MONASTICISM

No institution is more typical of mediæval religion than monasticism, and none had a more profound influence on religious life and thought. Originating in Egypt at the close of the third century, it spread with extraordinary rapidity throughout the Christian world. Nevertheless, at the time of the fall of the Empire it still possessed a somewhat exotic character in the west, and the monasteries of Southern Gaul and the Riviera, the chief centre of western monasticism, adhered very closely to their Egyptian and Oriental models. These Egyptian traditions and ideals were popularized above all by John Cassian, the Abbot of St Victor, at Marseilles (*c.* 360-435) whose writings had an extraordinary influence throughout the Middle Ages. The influence of this South Gallic monasticism, especially that of the school of Lerins, reached the British Isles at a very early date and inspired the great movement of Celtic monasticism in the sixth and seventh centuries. Meanwhile, however, in Southern Italy a specifically Latin form of monastic life was being created by St Benedict, which was destined to become the classical type of monasticism throughout the Western Church. Its characteristic notes are its moderation and its corporate spirit, in contrast to the individualism and the extreme asceticism which were characteristic alike of Oriental and Celtic monasticism. Throughout the Dark Ages the influence of the Benedictine rule steadily increased, first in England, thanks to St Gregory and his successors, then, through the Anglo-Saxon Benedictine missionaries, in Germany, and finally throughout the Carolingian Empire, where it finally became officially recognised as the standard form of the monastic life.

By this time, however, the monastery had changed its character. It was no longer, as in Egypt, a community of ascetics who had cut themselves off from all contact with the world. It had become a great social institution, a centre of education and learning, owning vast tracts of country and ruling the lives of a great dependent population. This type of social monasticism was dominant from the eighth to the twelfth centuries, and retained its importance down to the end of the Middle Ages. Its best examples are to be seen in the great Carolingian abbeys, such as Fulda and Corbie, Reichenau and St Gall, which were the chief and almost the only centres of culture in the ninth and tenth centuries. The wealth and power of these monasteries, however, inevitably tended to secularize them. Emperors and princes often treated them as rewards to bestow on their supporters, or as public offices in the administration of the Empire, while the anarchy that followed the fall of the Carolingian Empire produced still more serious abuses. Rich abbeys were treated as plunder, and every successful swashbuckler who established a feudal principality appropriated not only the monastic property, but the very office of Abbot. Thus the Count of Poitou was *ex officio* Abbot of St Hilary of Poitiers, while Hugh Capet was simultaneously abbot of four great monasteries. The reaction against these abuses, which began in the tenth century, is the turning point of the Middle Ages, and marks the beginning of that revival of western culture of which I have already spoken. At Cluny, in Burgundy, and in the monasteries of Lorraine there began a movement of reform and of return to the strict observance of the Benedictine rule, which spread rapidly through Western Europe, including England (St Dunstan). In the eleventh century this reformed monasticism provided the driving force of the wider movement of ecclesiastical reform, and had an immense influence on western culture. Almost all the leaders of the Church in that age—Gregory VII, Urban II, Peter Damian, Cardinal Humbert, St Hugh of Cluny, Lanfranc, St Anselm—were Benedictines who brought the spirit of monastic reform into the secularized and feudalized Church of the eleventh century. But it is in the Cistercian Order, and in its greatest representative, St Bernard, that we see mediæval monasticism in its fullest development. The Cistercian reform preserved the ascetic spirit and the contemplative ideal of the older monasticism, but at the same time it treated the monastery not as an end in itself, but as part of a wider unity—the Order—a great corporation which transcended the limits of diocese and kingdom, and reflected in its constitution the international character of the reformed mediæval Church.

With the thirteenth century, however, the religious life assumes an entirely new form, with the coming of the Franciscans and the other mendicant orders. In contrast to the Cluniac and Cistercian reforms,

St Francis went back behind the whole monastic movement to the New Testament, and substituted the apostolic life of preaching and teaching for the ascetic and liturgical ideals of the older monastic orders. The new orders could devote themselves to the service of the Church and of the poor without any of the restrictions which limited the external activities of the monk to his cloister. This principle of the socialization of the religious life in the service of the Church marks an epoch in the history of Christendom, since it is typical not only of the Franciscans and the Dominicans, but also of the post-Reformation orders, such as the Jesuits, which have played such an important part in the history of the modern Church. If the early Middle Ages were the age of the monks, the later Middle Ages are the age of the Friars, and their action is to be seen not only in their missionary activity, but intellectually in the universities and in the development of scholasticism, and spiritually in their influence on the great mystical movement of the fourteenth century, and the new forms of piety and popular devotion. Their influence was especially strong in Italy during the period of the early Renaissance, through such saints and religious leaders as St Catherine and St Bernardino of Siena, St Antonino of Florence, and Savonarola. In fact, their action did much to save the religious life of Italy from the secularizing influence of the Renaissance culture, and thus to prepare the way for the religious revival of the Counter-Reformation.

THE PAPACY

If monasticism was one of the main formative influences in mediæval religion, the Papacy was the other; and it was the alliance of these two forces from the time of St Gregory the Great onwards which did more than anything else to create mediæval culture. Nevertheless, Rome itself was far from being the centre of mediæval culture. That culture developed rather on the basis of the Frankish monarchy and the Carolingian Empire. It had its centre in the north, in the lands between the Rhine and the Rhone and the Loire, while Rome remained for many centuries in closer touch with the Byzantine East than with the Frankish North.

The fall of the Empire in the West had, in fact, left the Papacy in a somewhat anomalous position. By tradition and canon law, it was the head of the Church of the Empire, the greatest of the Apostolic sees and the first of the patriarchates. It still enjoyed a unique prestige in the east as the See of Peter, and in every great controversy from Arianism to

Iconoclasm it was appealed to by the orthodox party in the east as the defender of the faith. But at the same time the growing divorce between Byzantine East and the Latin and barbarian West left Rome isolated between two worlds. The real ruler of the Church of the Empire was not the Roman Pope but the Byzantine Emperor, and the reconquest of Italy by Justinian threatened to reduce the Papacy to abject dependence on the Cæsaropapism of the imperial court. From this fate Rome was saved, on the one hand, by the renewed collapse of the Empire after the death of Justinian, and on the other by the initiative of Gregory the Great and his successors in the conversion of the barbarians and the creation of a new western Christendom. Thus during the Dark Ages the Papacy underwent a gradual reorientation from the Byzantine east to the Germanic north. The turning point came in the eighth century with the conversion of Germany by St Boniface, acting as the legate of the Holy See, and with the breach between Rome and the Byzantine Empire on the Iconoclast controversy. It finds a clear expression in the famous letters of Gregory II to Leo III, in which he defies the Emperor to do his worst and appeals to the new peoples of the west, who are ready to shed their blood in defence of St Peter and the Holy See.[1]

---

[1]The genuineness of these letters has been questioned in the past but it has recently been vindicated by the latest historian of the Papacy, E. Caspar, *Geschichte des Papstums* II.

The result of this change was to be seen in that alliance between the Papacy and the Frankish kingdom, which was sealed in 754, on the one hand by the solemn anointing of Pepin by Pope Stephan II as King of the Franks and, on the other, by "the donation of Pepin," which placed the remnants of Roman territory in Italy under the Papal sovereignty and thus laid the foundation of the States of the Church. But this did not really secure the independence of the Holy See, since the growth of the Frankish power threatened it with fresh dangers, and the new Christian Empire of Charles the Great was inspired by the same Cæsaropapist ideal as that of the Byzantine state. Nevertheless, the situation in the West was essentially different from that in the East. There the Empire stood, so to speak, on its own feet, and was able to incorporate the Church in the fixed *cadres* of its bureaucratic organization. In the West, on the other hand, the Church was older and more firmly organized than the new Carolingian State. In fact the latter was itself the product of the pre-existing ecclesiastical unity.

Consequently, when the new Empire began to decline, the Papacy naturally stepped into its place as the leader of the Christian people and the supreme authority of Christendom. Thus the Pontificate of Nicholas I (858-867) already foreshadows the great age of the mediæval papacy, when the Holy See acquired a theocratic character which involved the subordination to it of the temporal power. At the same time the episcopate came to rely more and more upon the Papacy against the growing power of the metropolitans, like Hincmar of Rheims, who wished to reduce the episcopate to almost complete dependence on themselves, and it was as part of this reaction—*i.e.*, in order to protect the rights of the episcopate against the metropolitans, and against the secular power—that the False Decretals were composed in the West Frankish kingdom during the second half of the ninth century.

The age of Nicholas I was, however, separated from the age of Gregory VII and his successors by a dark period of almost 200 years, during which the Papacy fell a victim to the ambition of the Roman nobles, and was used as a power in the party struggles of the local oligarchy. It was not until the Christian Empire had been revived by the German emperors, and the morale of the Church had been restored by the work of the monastic reformers that it was possible for the Papacy to realize the ideals of Nicholas I, and to secure the independence of the Holy See and its effective supremacy in western Christendom. The decisive step was taken by Nicholas II in 1059, when he laid down the conditions for the election of the Pope and confined the right of participation to the Roman clergy—the "cardinals."[1] The full programme of the reforming party is to be found in the *Dictatus Papæ*, a memorandum drawn up by Gregory VII in May, 1075. But in addition to the classical doctrines of the divine origin and authority of the Holy See, its infallibility and its rights as the supreme court of appeal and the final authority in jurisdiction and doctrine, we find a new assertion of the political rights of the Pope—the right to depose emperors and to release subjects from their allegiance to unjust princes. These were the claims that had emerged in the course of the struggle with the Empire, and their assertion is one of the most characteristic features of the later mediæval Papacy, above all in the period between Gregory VII and Boniface VIII. We cannot understand them unless we remember the peculiar character of the mediæval state, which had its origin with Charles the Great, and which had been restored and continued by the Germanic emperors. It was not so much a secular state in our sense of the word, as the temporal organ of a spiritual society. As the canonist, Stephan of Tournai, remarks: "In the same city, and under the same King, there are two peoples and two authorities. The city is the Church, the King is

---

[1] Originally to the cardinal bishops only.

Christ, the two peoples are the clergy and the laity, and the two authorities are the priesthood and the kingship."[1] Now if we regard Christian society in this way as an undivided unity, it is clear that the ultimate authority will be the spiritual one, and that the temporal power will be regarded as its minister in earthly matters and will possess only a delegated authority.

It is true that the imperialist partisans contested this, since they regarded the emperor as the true head of Christendom. Nevertheless, they accepted the same unitary conception of Christian society—indeed it is with them rather than with the Popes that this idea originated—and consequently their claims on behalf of the State amounted not to the independence of the secular power in its own province but to the right of the emperor as the anointed ruler of the Christian people to control the Church as well as the State and to be, like the Byzantine Emperor, the head of the two hierarchies of the civil and ecclesiastical orders. It is obvious that these conceptions both of them involve a certain confusion between the functions of the temporal and spiritual powers. It is indeed inaccurate to describe the resultant conflicts as due to the theocratic claims of the Papacy, since the Imperialist position is equally theocratic. Nor was it

---

[1] Stephan of Tournai, cited by Carlyle, *History of Mediæval Political Theory*, ii. 198, and iv. 166.

a struggle between Church and State in the modern sense, since both parties assumed the existence of a common social unity—a Church-State of the Christian people.

If we accept these premises it is clear that the Papacy was far better equipped for the task of common leadership, even in temporal matters, than was the Holy Roman Empire which, for all its universal claims, remained a local Central European power. Consequently, so long as the unitary conception of mediæval society endured—that is to say from the time of Gregory VII to Boniface VIII—we find the Papacy fulfilling a dual task as head of the Church and as leader and judge of Christian society in its widest aspect; and the greatest of the mediæval Popes—men such as Gregory VII, Urban II, and Innocent III— were not unequal to the immense burden that was laid upon them, as we see from the record of their many-sided activities that is contained in the Papal Registers. Nevertheless, this state of things could not survive in the changed political atmosphere which resulted from the constitutional development of mediæval society and the formation of the new national monarchies. The State became conscious of its independent aims and functions, and this process was facilitated, by the neo-Aristotelianism of St Thomas, which gave the State an independent basis in nature and reason. Thus the later centuries of the Middle Ages saw the liquidation of the unitary conception of Christian society and of the theocratic ideals that had accompanied it. The defeat of the theocratic Empire by the Papacy was followed by the defeat of the theocratic Papacy by the national monarchies. The latter, however, still preserved a great deal of the older tradition. It is only in Renaissance Italy that we find the new ideas applied logically and consistently to political and ecclesiastical problems. Elsewhere the State retained a semi-theocratic character which found expression in the new Gallican theories and in that doctrine of the Divine Right of Kings, which played so large a part at the Reformation and in post-Reformation times. Not content with depriving the Papacy of the quasi-political functions that it had possessed in the unitary society of the mediæval Church-State, it attacked its apostolic authority as the divinely-ordained head of the Church, and set up instead the new ideal of a State-Church under the control of the secular power. Unfortunately, during this period the Papacy was weakened, first by its removal from Rome to Avignon, then by the Great Schism, and finally by the secularizing influence of the Renaissance. Consequently, it was not until the age of the Counter-Reformation and the Council of Trent that the Papacy was able fully to reassert its authority as the ruler of an autonomous spiritual society, which was distinct both in its end and its functions from the secular society of the State.

HERESY AND THE INQUISITION

The Middle Ages began and ended in a tempest of heresy and schism. They began in the age of the great Christological controversies, when the Christian East became Monophysite, or Nestorian; and they ended in the age of the Reformation, when Northern Europe became Protestant. Between these two points, however, heresy played a comparatively small part in Western Europe, and one of the most striking features of mediæval civilization is its religious unity. The Latin Church was hardly affected, except in its external relations, by the Christological controversies, and the characteristic Western heresies of the Patristic age, such as Novatianism and Donatism, were concerned with moral and disciplinary questions rather than with matters of dogma. Even Pelagianism, the most theological of the western heresies, was more concerned with the problem of moral responsibility than with the esoteric theological problems that absorbed the mind of the Christian East. Moreover, these heresies hardly survived the fall of the Empire.

In the following age, the great enemy of Catholicism was not heresy but paganism, and the issues which divided Christians were matters of ritual rather than of dogma, as we see in the case of the Paschal controversy in the Celtic Churches, or the question of the Azymes—the use of unleavened bread in the liturgy—which assumed so great an importance in the relations between the Greek East and the Latin West.

No doubt the schism between the Eastern and Western Churches which was finally consummated in the eleventh century, involved purely theological questions such as the Dual Procession of the Holy Spirit, but the schism did not affect the interior life of western Christendom save in so far as it strengthened its own unity and cohesion against the outer world.

The revival of western culture in the eleventh century was, however, accompanied by a new heretical movement which, in the following two centuries, grew to be a serious danger to Catholicism. This was the Catharist movement, and it should perhaps be regarded not so much as a heresy as a rival religion, since it was rooted in the non-Christian and perhaps pre-Christian dualism of the ancient East, which was transmitted to the West, through the Balkan peninsula, by the Paulicians and the Bogomils. In any case, it is of the greatest importance for the history of mediæval religion, and we cannot understand the latter unless we realize that the alternative to Catholicism was not some form of simplified or rationalized Christianity, but a religion which regarded the body and the whole material world as the creation of Satan, and which condemned marriage and child-bearing as essentially sinful. It was forbidden for the Catharist not only to marry, but to kill any living thing, or to eat anything that was the fruit of sexual generation. But this life of strict asceticism belonged only to the "perfect," who had received the *consolamentum*, "the baptism with the spirit and with fire," which was the great sacrament of the Catharist religion. The ordinary Catharist was merely a "believer" who shared neither the privileges nor the privations of the "perfect," through whom alone they could hope to attain contact with the spiritual world. Thus Catharism combined extreme asceticism with considerable laxity, and even antinomianism in practice.

It is not surprising that a heresy of so fundamental a nature, which regarded the God of the Catholics as an evil power and the Church itself as the creation of Satan, should have been met with remorseless persecution and repression. Indeed, the rise of Catharism in Western Europe seems to have been largely responsible for the new attitude to heresy and persecution which marked the later mediæval Church. Hitherto, it is true, the Church had regarded the suppression of heresy as part of the duty of the State, but it had shown itself averse from extreme measures, and the sentence "Ecclesia abhorret a sanguine" had been accepted as an established maxim. But the Catharists were in an entirely different category to other heretics. They were regarded alike by pagans and Christians as enemies of the human race. Even before the advent of Christianity, Manichaeism was treated as a capital offence by Roman law, and the Byzantine Empire had attempted to exterminate the Paulicians with fire and sword. Consequently the execution of the first western Cathari by King Robert of France, in 1022, was by no means such an innovation as it is usually supposed to be, but was merely the first appearance in the west of the traditional Roman and Byzantine practice. Owing, however, to the intimate fusion of Church and State in the unitary society of Christendom, which I have described in the previous section, it became increasingly difficult for the Church to avoid responsibility for such acts, though the leaders of orthodox opinion, such as St Bernard and Gerhoh of Reichersberg, continued to maintain the older views. When the Church had taken the lead in preaching the Crusade against the infidel abroad, it seemed inconsistent to condemn the use of the sword against the heretic at home. Accordingly, in the second half of the twelfth century we find a growing movement in favour of a crusade against the Catharists, which came to a head in the crusade against the Albigenses in 1208. Nevertheless, though Innocent III, under the influence of Roman law, had assimilated heresy to the crime of High Treason (*laesa majestate*) for which the penalty was death, he still stopped short of the death penalty, and only decreed exile and confiscation in the anti-heretical legislature of the Fourth Lateran Council.

The final step seems to have been taken in consequence of the action of that brilliant and sinister figure, Frederick II, who covered his own doubtful orthodoxy by the zeal with which he persecuted heretics and the ruthlessness of his anti-heretical legislation. It is probable that his action was due to a desire to assert his authority in religious matters at the expense of the ecclesiastical authority. In any case the Pope (Gregory IX) was unwilling to leave the "inquisition" of heretics to the civil power, and he accordingly appointed special commissioners for the purpose in 1231, which may be regarded as the date of the official foundation of the Inquisition. Both the legislation of Frederick and that of the Popes was affected by the influence of the revived Roman Law as, for example, in the use of judicial torture, which was the worst feature of the new procedure. This marks a serious breach with the older mediæval tradition, for the Church had opposed the use of torture not only in patristic times, but in the darkest period of the Dark Ages, when Pope Nicholas I had argued forcibly on its essential folly and injustice, in his letter to the converted Bulgarians. Here the attitude of the Dark Ages seems more enlightened than that of the later mediæval and Renaissance periods, and the same is true of the belief in witchcraft, which was opposed as a relic of pagan superstition by Nicholas I and Agobard, and the ecclesiastical advisers of Charlemagne,[1] but which spread like a contagion throughout Europe at the close of the Middle Ages and reached its height in the post-Reformation period.

---

[1] So, too, Gregory VII had warned King Haakon of Denmark against the persecution of witches, "Learn rather," he writes, "to turn away the wrath of God by worthy penance, than to provoke His anger yet further by useless savagery against these innocents." *Register ed. Caspar* ii. 498.

The close of the patristic period and the early part of the Middle Ages was the creative age of liturgy in the west. They saw the formation and development of the different liturgical traditions which were characteristic of the different parts of Europe. The Roman liturgy in Southern and Central Italy, the Ambrosian liturgy of Milan and Lombardy, the Gothic or Mozarabic rite in Spain, and the Gallican liturgies north of the Alps.[1] At first sight this diversity seems strange in contrast to the uniformity of the East, where each patriarchate has its own liturgy. But it is, after all, the natural result of the conditions in the West after the fall of the Empire, when the Church in each of the barbarian kingdoms lived a comparatively independent and isolated life, and relations with Rome were loose and intermittent. Under these circumstances it was natural that the Church of the Visigothic kingdom should look to Toledo, and that of the Lombard kingdom to Milan, while Arles occupied a similar position in the Church of Gaul in the sixth century. But in spite of this independence and diversity, there was no lack of mutual influences. The Byzantine

---

[1]We may also mention the African liturgy, the oldest Latin liturgy of all, which we only know indirectly through the writings of St Augustine, etc., and the Celtic liturgies, which were of a very composite character and show both Roman and Gallican influences.

liturgy influenced that of Rome, which itself formed part of the Byzantine Empire from the sixth to the eighth centuries. Rome influenced the other western Churches, while the latter also show traces of direct oriental (*i.e.*, Byzantine) influences.

Thus the liturgical development at the beginning of the Middle Ages was centrifugal, and the Roman liturgy, for which we possess by far the fullest and earliest evidence, followed an independent and specifically Roman line of evolution which acquired a definitive form between the fifth and the seventh centuries.

In the seventh century, however, there began a process of expansion which continued at intervals throughout the Middle Ages, and finally ended in the sixteenth century with the establishment of almost complete liturgical uniformity in the West.[1] Thus as early as the time of St Gregory, the Benedictine missionaries began to introduce the Roman liturgy into England, where it was finally established by the Synods of Whitby and Cloveshoe. From England it was brought back to the Continent by St Boniface, and through his influence, and later through that of Alcuin and the other religious advisers of Charles the Great, it became the official rite of the Carolingian Empire. Here, however, it became blended with

---

[1]The exceptions are Milan, Toledo, Lyons, and certain religious orders, notably the Dominicans.

Gallican elements, and this mixed Gallo-Roman rite in turn reacted on that of Rome itself during the following centuries. Thus the Middle Ages witnessed a gradual process of fusion and syncretism between the western rites, under the guidance and predominance of Rome. From the Gallican liturgies we have received the elaborate ceremonial of the Paschal liturgy, the use of proses and sequences and the introduction of the Creed in the Mass, which was borrowed from the East by Spain, in the sixth century, and then passed to Gaul, finally reaching Rome in the eleventh century by way of Germany.

Thus the unity of our existing liturgy is part of the legacy of the Middle Ages, and corresponds to the rich diversity in unity of mediæval Christendom. This liturgical development was accompanied by a corresponding growth of devotion to the Sacrament of the Altar. Frequent communion was rare during the Middle Ages, and many of the saints only made their communion on the greater feasts. On the other hand, attendance at Mass grew more and more frequent until, in the thirteenth century, pious laymen like King Henry III would hear as many as three High Masses every day. On one occasion, when his cousin, St Louis, urged him to go and hear a sermon instead, he is said to have replied that he who has a dear friend far prefers to see him than to hear other people talk about him. It was in order to satisfy this desire that the practice of elevating the Host after the consecration was introduced about this time, and that by the fourteenth century the Holy Sacrament was exposed to public veneration, both on the altar and in solemn processions like those of Corpus Christi, the new feast which had been instituted in honour of the Holy Sacrament in 1264.

The Middle Ages also saw a very important development in the administration of the Sacrament of Penance. The discipline of public penance for grave sins (such as apostasy, fornication, and homicide) which had been a characteristic feature of Western Catholicism in the Patristic Age gradually disappeared and the administration of the sacrament became entirely private. This change was accompanied by a more frequent use of the sacrament and was reflected in the decree of the Fourth Council of the Lateran in 1215, which laid down the duty of annual auricular confession.

A number of different factors contributed to this change. The old system of public penance was, as we have said, restricted to cases of very grave sin, and it involved proportionately serious consequences, since the penitent, even after absolution, was forbidden to marry, to bear arms, or to engage in commerce. Nor could it ever be repeated, so that the relapsed penitent remained excommunicated. The severity of this discipline explains why so many believers in the early centuries postponed their baptism, as did Constantine the Great, to the end of their lives. It can never have been an easy system to administer, and in the anarchy and violence of the dark ages it became absolutely impossible. At the same time the growth of monasticism led to the development of spiritual direction and the need for frequent confession of lesser faults. The old system was suited neither to the lower standards of the barbarian converts nor to the higher standards of the monks. Consequently, its place was gradually taken by new forms of penitential discipline. This system developed especially in the predominantly monastic Celtic churches, and was diffused throughout the Continent by the Celtic and Anglo-Saxon Penitentials, which represent an intermediate stage between the ancient and the modern systems[1] In the Carolingian age we find private confession becoming the normal practice,

---

[1] The Anglo-Saxon Penitential of Theodore expressly states that no regulation is made for the public reconciliation of penitents because there is no public penance in this province, while the Dialogue of Egbert, the eighth century Archbishop of York, recalls that the custom has obtained in the English Church from the time of Theodore and Pope Vitalian, that not only the clergy in the monasteries, but also laymen with their wives and families should resort to their confessors and do penance during the twelve days before Christmas, Haddan and Stubbs *Councils* iii. 413

for example, St Chrodegang of Metz lays down in his rule that the clergy should make their confession to the bishop at least twice a year, and Alcuin, above all, insists on the duty of confession for clergy and laity alike. Nevertheless, Alcuin himself[1] states that in Aquitaine the practice of confession was confined to the monks, and the disorder and corruption of the following period was unfavourable to any general progress. Coincident with the increase of confession we find the curious practice of confession to a layman, in the absence of a priest, which was especially prevalent during the reforming movement of the eleventh and twelfth centuries, and was also known, and to some extent recognised, by Albert the Great and St Thomas Aquinas in the thirteenth century (St Thomas explains that a layman cannot really absolve[2]). The decree of the Lateran Council put an end to the vagueness and uncertainty that had existed in the period of transition, and during the later Middle Ages the influence of the friars as confessors and directors and moral theologians had an immense influence on the development of more frequent confession, and the importance of the sacrament of penance in the religious life of the people.

---

[1] Ep. 112 in *Migne*, vol. c.
[2] *Summa Theol.*, III, Supp. b., q. 8, art. 2, ad. 1.

BIBLIOGRAPHY

GENERAL:

Schnurer, *Kirche und Kultur im Mittelalter*, 3 vols., 1927, etc.

P. Pourrat, *La Spiritualité Chrétienne*, vol. ii., *Le Moyen Age*, 1924 (English translation).

F. Vernet, *La spiritualité médiévale*, 1929 (English translation in the Catholic Library of Religious Knowledge).

P. Rousselot (and J. Huby), *Le christianisme du moyen-âge*, in *Christus: Manuel d'histoire des religions*, a brilliant essay. English adaption by Fr. d'Arcy: *The Life of the Church*, 1933.

C. Dawson, *The Making of Europe* (to A.D. 1000), 1932; *Religion and the Rise of Western Civilisation*, 1950; *Mediæval Essays*, 1953.

C. Butler, *Western Mysticism*, 2nd edition, 1927.

R. Garrigou-Lagrange, O.P., *Christian Perfection and Contemplation*, 1939: *The Three Ages of the Interior Life* (1951).

MONASTICISM:

C. Butler, *Benedictine Monachism*, 1924 (2nd edition).

U. Berlière, *L'ordre monastique*, 3rd edition, 1924.

Montalembert, *The Monks of the West* (English translation, edited by Cardinal Gasquet, 6 vols., 1896), uncritical but a classic.

J. Ryan, *Irish Monasticism*, 1931.

D. Knowles, *The Monastic Order in England*, 1940 (943-1216).

D. Knowles, *The Religious Orders in England*, 1948 (1216-1340).

THE PAPACY:

H. Grisar, *Rome and the Popes in the Early Middle Ages* (from Constantine to Gregory I), 3 vols., illustrated, 1911.

P. Hughes, *History of the Church*, vols. II and III, 1947-8.

Histoire de l'Eglise, ed. Fliche et Martin (16 vols. published, reaching to 1878).

L. Duchesne, *Les premiers temps de l'Etat Pontifical*, 3rd edition, 1914.

J. Gay, *Les Papes du XI siècle et la chrétienté*, 1926.

A. Fliche, *La réforme grégorienne*, 2 vols., 1924, etc.

J. Rivière, *La problème de l'Eglise et de l'Etat au temps de Philippe le Bel*, 1926.

HERESY AND THE INQUISITION:

E. Vacandard, *L'Inquisition*, 2nd edition, 1913 (English translation, 1908, from 1st edition).

J. Guiraud, *L'Inquisition médiévale*, 1928. (English translation by E. Messenger).

A. S. Turberville, *Mediæval Heresy and the Inquisition*, 1920.

LITURGY:

F. Cabrol, *The Mass in the West*, 1934; *The Books of the Latin Liturgy*, 1932 (in the Catholic Library of Religious Knowledge).

L. Duchesne, *Christian Worship, its origin and evolution* (English translation, 5th edition, 1919).

A. Fortescue, *The Mass*, 3rd edition, 1937.

H. Thurston, *Lent and Holy Week*, 1904.

BRITISH ISLES:

L. Gougaud, *Christianity in Celtic Lands*. (London, 1932.)

St Bede, *The Ecclesiastical History of the English People* (a great book by a great saint. There are several English translations).

W. Levison, *England and the Continent in the Eighth Century*, 1946.

Z. N. Brooke, *The English Church and the Papacy from the Conquest to the Reign of John* (1931).

F. W. Maitland, *Roman Canon Law in the Church of England*, 1898 (Methuen).

C. H. Talbot, *The Anglo Saxon Missionaries in Germany*, 1954 (The Makers of Christendom Series).

MEDIÆVAL THOUGHT:

D. J. B. Hawkins, *A Sketch of Mediæval Philosophy* (1947).

R. W. and A. J. Carlyle, *A History of Mediæval Political Theory in the West*, 1903-1936, 6 vols.

F. Copleston, S.J., *A History of Philosophy*. vol. ii, Augustine to Scotus (1950); vol. iii, Ockham to Suarez (1953).

Mediæval Philosophy (Home Study Books, 1952).

E. Gilson, *History of Christian Philosophy in the Middle Ages*, 1955 (Sheed & Ward).

BACKGROUND

In a broad survey of a thousand years of religious history, Christopher Dawson stresses the non-European roots of mediæval Christendom, but also its flourishing in lands beyond the frontiers of classical civilisation. This marriage of Mediterranean and near-Eastern culture with the barbarian peoples of the North was fruitful in myriad ways: classical culture was preserved, the rule of law established (in theory at least) and the expression of Christianity in theology, philosophy, literature and architecture flourished. Social norms benefitted from Christian influence, and the great monasteries became oases of learning and a power in the land. He traces with care the fascinating development of the Roman liturgy. Above all, Dawson explains how for a time the whole creative and social current of Europe was infused with Christianity, and its monuments – literary, architectural, legal and social – all form part of the patrimony both of Christendom and of world civilisation.

CTS ONEFIFTIES

1. FR DAMIEN & WHERE ALL ROADS LEAD · *Robert Louis Stevenson & G K Chesterton*

2. THE UNENDING CONFLICT · *Hilaire Belloc*

3. CHRIST UPON THE WATERS · *John Henry Newman*

4. DEATH & RESURRECTION · *Leonard Cheshire VC & Bede Jarrett OP*

5. THE DAY THE BOMB FELL · *Johannes Siemes SJ & Bruce Kent*

6. MIRACLES · *Ronald Knox*

7. A CITY SET ON A HILL · *Robert Hugh Benson*

8. FINDING THE WAY BACK · *Francis Ripley*

9. THE GUNPOWDER PLOT · *Herbert Thurston SJ*

10. NUNS – WHAT ARE THEY FOR? · *Maria Boulding OSB, Bruno Webb OSB & Jean Cardinal Daniélou SJ*

11. ISLAM, BRITAIN & THE GOSPEL · *John Coonan, William Burridge & John Wijngaards*

12. STORIES OF THE GREAT WAR · *Eileen Boland*

13. LIFE WITHIN US · *Caryll Houselander, Delia Smith & Herbert Fincham*

14. INSIDE COMMUNISM · *Douglas Hyde*

15. COURTSHIP: SOME PRACTICAL ADVICE · *Anon, Hubert McEvoy SJ, Tony Kirwin & Malcolm Brennan*

16. RESURRECTION · *Vincent McNabb OP & B C Butler OSB*

17. TWO CONVERSION STORIES · *James Britten & Ronald Knox*

18. MEDIEVAL CHRISTIANITY · *Christopher Dawson*

19. A LIBRARY OF TALES – VOL 1 · *Lady Herbert of Lea*

20. A LIBRARY OF TALES – VOL 2 · *Eveline Cole & E Kielty*

21. WAR AT HOME AND AT THE FRONT · *"A Chaplain" & Mrs Blundell of Crosby*

22. THE CHURCH & THE MODERN AGE · *Christopher Hollis*

23. THE PRAYER OF ST THÉRÈSE OF LISIEUX · *Vernon Johnson*

24. THE PROBLEM OF EVIL · *Martin D'Arcy SJ*

25. WHO IS ST JOSEPH? · *Herbert Cardinal Vaughan*